WASHINGTON TEST PREP

Reading and Writing

Common Core Workbook

Grade 3

ISBN 978-1507786123

CONTENTS

INTRODUCTION
For Parents, Teachers, and Tutors

Developing Common Core Reading and Writing Skills

The state of Washington has adopted the Common Core State Standards. These standards describe what students are expected to know. Students will be instructed based on these standards and the Smarter Balanced, or SBAC, assessments will include questions based on these standards. This workbook will develop the Common Core reading and writing skills that students are expected to have, while preparing students for the state tests and giving students practice completing a range of reading and writing tasks. The emphasis in this workbook is on writing skills, but complementary reading skills are also covered as students complete tasks involving providing written answers to reading comprehension questions.

Completing Practice Sets

This workbook is divided into 10 practice sets. Each practice set includes four tasks that progress from simple to more complex. The types of tasks are described below.

Task Type	Details
Short Passage with Questions	These tasks contain a short passage followed by reading comprehension questions requiring written answers. They also include a Core Writing Skills Practice exercise that focuses on one key writing skill. These exercises may require students to respond to a text, complete a research project, or complete a writing task.
Long Passage with Essay Question	These tasks contain a long passage followed by an essay question requiring a written answer of 1 to 2 pages. They also include hints and planning guidance to help students develop effective writing skills.
Personal Narrative Writing Task	These tasks contain a writing prompt for a personal narrative, as well as hints and planning guidance.
Short Story Writing Task	These tasks contain a writing prompt for a story, as well as hints and planning guidance.
Opinion Piece Writing Task	These tasks contain a writing prompt for an opinion piece, as well as hints and planning guidance.
Explanatory Writing Task	These tasks contain a writing prompt for an essay, as well as hints and planning guidance.

By completing the practice sets, students will have experience with all types of Common Core writing tasks. This includes writing in response to passages, writing all the types of texts covered in the Common Core standards, gathering information from sources, and completing research projects.

Some of the writing tasks also include guides for editing and revising completed work. This encourages students to review their work and improve on it, while the checklists help ensure that students focus on the key criteria that work is judged on. This will help prepare students for the writing tasks found on assessments, as well as guide students on the key features of strong student writing.

Preparing for the SBAC English Language Arts/Literacy Assessments

Students will be assessed each year by taking a set of tests known as the Smarter Balanced, or SBAC, assessments. Strong writing skills are essential for performing well on the SBAC assessments. The assessments include reading comprehension questions requiring written answers, research tasks, and writing tasks where students write essays, opinion pieces, and narratives.

This workbook will help prepare students for the SBAC assessments. The questions and exercises will develop the more advanced Common Core skills, provide extensive experience providing written answers, and help students learn to write effective essays, opinion pieces, and narratives. This will ensure that students have the skills and experience they need to perform well on the SBAC assessments.

Reading and Writing

Practice Set 1

This practice set contains four writing tasks. These are described below.

Task 1: Short Passage with Questions

This task has a short passage followed by questions. Read each question carefully. Then write your answer in the space provided.

You can also practice writing skills by completing the Core Writing Skills Practice exercise.

Task 2: Short Passage with Questions

This task has a short passage followed by questions. Read each question carefully. Then write your answer in the space provided.

You can also practice writing skills by completing the Core Writing Skills Practice exercise.

Task 3: Long Passage with Essay Question

This task has a longer passage with an essay question. Read the passage, complete the planning page, and then write or type your answer.

Task 4: Personal Narrative Writing Task

This final task requires you to write a personal narrative. Read the writing prompt, complete the planning page, and then write or type your answer.

Task 1: Short Passage with Questions

Finland

Finland is a country at the top of Europe. The total area of Finland is over 130,000 square miles. This makes Finland the eighth largest country in Europe. Its neighbors are Sweden, Norway, and Russia.

The capital of Finland is Helsinki. Helsinki is home to nearly 540,000 people. Finland's population as a whole is just over 5 million.

People in Finland most commonly speak Finnish or Swedish. Sometimes they will speak both.

CORE WRITING SKILLS PRACTICE

The passage states that Finland is the eighth largest country in Europe. Use the Internet to find the top ten largest countries in Europe. List the top ten largest countries in Europe in order.

1. _____

2. _____

3. _____

4. _____

5. _____

6. _____

7. _____

8. _Finland_

9. _____

10. _____

---

1 Complete the chart with **three** more facts given about Finland.

Hint A fact is something that can be proven to be true.

It has a population of just over 5 million.			

Finland

2 What information from the passage does the map best support?

Hint Read through all the details in the passage. Focus on finding the details that are also shown on the map.

_____

_____

_____

_____

_____

Task 2: Short Passage with Questions

Busy Bees

There are twenty thousand known species of bees in the world. Different types of honey bees make up only seven of those species.

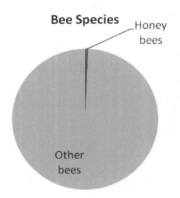

Bee Species

Honey bees

Other bees

The honey bee is believed to have come from South East Asia. However, scientists believe that some species could have come from Europe.

Today, honey bees are used by beekeepers to help pollinate crops of flowers. They are also used to make honey and to make beeswax.

Bees feed on the nectar and pollen found in flowers. As they move from flower to flower, they spread the pollen. This process pollinates flowers.

CORE WRITING SKILLS PRACTICE

Which paragraph from the passage does the information in the box most relate to? Explain how the information in the box relates to the paragraph.

_____

_____

_____

_____

_____

1   The web below lists one use of bees. Complete the web by listing **two** more uses of bees mentioned in the passage.

 **Hint**   When answering questions like this, make sure you use information that is given in the passage. Only list uses of bees that are mentioned in the passage.

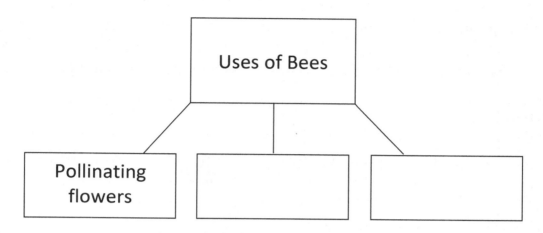

2   Describe what the graph shows about the number of species of honey bees.

_____

_____

_____

_____

_____

_____

Task 3: Long Passage with Essay Question

Directions: Read the passage below. Then answer the question that follows. Use the planning page to plan your writing. Then write or type your essay.

Playing a Musical Instrument

Playing a musical instrument is a popular pastime for all age ranges. Young or old, it is lots of fun to play a musical instrument. There are many different types to choose from including guitar, piano, trumpet, and saxophone.

Making a Choice

First, you need to choose a musical instrument that you would like to learn how to play. Here are some things you should think about:

- the cost of the instrument
- how easy or difficult the instrument is to learn
- whether there is a teacher available to help you learn it
- what opportunities there will be to play it

Getting Your Gear

Now you have chosen your instrument, you need to buy it. If it is expensive, you might like to borrow it instead. That way, you can make sure it is the right choice before spending a lot of money.

Some schools will lend students instruments. Or perhaps you can look in your local paper or online for a secondhand instrument, which are usually much cheaper.

Getting Ready to Learn

After you have your instrument, you should then create a learning plan. This might involve private lessons with a music teacher or going to music classes. Some people choose to learn on their own. You can use books, movies, web sites, or you can even watch videos online.

To learn quickly, your plan may include a variety of learning methods. Make sure that you attend every lesson or study your books regularly. Also, be sure to practice what you have learned as this is the best way to develop your new skill.

Making Music

Once you have learned enough to play a song, you should start playing for people. It is a good idea to start with your family or friends. Or you might play for your music class. Once you become confident, you can then play for larger groups of people.

Keep Going

To become a good musician, you have to keep playing. Keep learning as much as you can and practice often. Challenge yourself to learn more difficult songs as well. As you learn more, you will become better and better. Some people even become good enough to play music as a career.

1 If you were going to play a musical instrument, what type would you choose and why? What would you do to learn to play? Use details from the passage in your answer.

In your answer, be sure to
- describe what musical instrument you would choose and why
- describe how you would learn to play
- use details from the passage in your answer
- write an answer of between 1 and 2 pages

Hint

The passage gives advice on how to choose a musical instrument, and describes how readers can learn to play. To answer this question, you should write about how you would use the information in a real situation. You should refer to the advice given in the passage. However, you do not have to use all the advice.

An essay that gets full marks will not just repeat all the advice given in the passage. To get full marks, you should show that you are analyzing the advice and deciding for yourself whether to take it. You should apply it to your particular situation. If you are going to follow a certain piece of advice, be sure to clearly explain why.

You can also add some of your own ideas. For example, you might have other ideas on what to consider when choosing a musical instrument, or other ideas on how you could learn to play.

Planning Page

Summary

Write a brief summary of what you are going to write about.

Supporting Details

Write down the facts, details, or examples you are going to include in your answer.

Outline

Write a plan for what you are going to write. Include the main points you want to cover and the order you will cover them.

Task 4: Personal Narrative Writing Task

Directions: Read the writing prompt below. Use the planning page to plan your writing. Then write or type your answer.

People have different tastes in food. There are some foods that people like and others that they dislike. Think about a time that you tried a food you disliked.

Write a composition describing a time when you tried a food you disliked. Describe how you tried the food, what you disliked about it, and what you did after deciding you disliked it.

Hint

Make sure you answer each part of the question. Remember that you need to include the following:
- how you tried the food
- what you disliked about the food
- what you did after finding out you disliked the food

When you write your outline, make sure that it covers all of the parts of the question.

Planning Page

Summary

Write a brief summary of what you are going to write about.

Outline

Write a plan for what you are going to write. Include the main points you want to cover and the order you will cover them.

Writing and Editing Checklist

After you finish writing your personal narrative, you can use this guide to review and edit your work. Use the questions as a guide to finding ways you can improve your work.

Writing Checklist

- ✓ Does your work have a strong opening? Does it introduce the topic and the main ideas well?
- ✓ Is your work well-organized? Is related information grouped together? Does each paragraph have one main idea?
- ✓ Does your work have an effective ending? Does it tie up the ideas well?
- ✓ Is your work focused? Are there any details that do not fit with your main ideas?
- ✓ Do your ideas flow well? Have you used words and phrases to link ideas well?
- ✓ Have you used strong words? Are there words that could be replaced with better ones?
- ✓ Have you used effective descriptions? Could your descriptions be improved?
- ✓ Have you used sensory details? Could you add more sensory details to help readers imagine what you are writing about?

Editing Checklist

- ✓ Have you used a variety of sentence structures? Are your sentences all written correctly?
- ✓ Is the grammar correct?
- ✓ Are all words spelled correctly? You can check the spelling of any words you are not sure of.
- ✓ Is punctuation used correctly?
- ✓ If dialogue is used, is it punctuated correctly?
- ✓ Are all words capitalized correctly?

Reading and Writing

Practice Set 2

This practice set contains four writing tasks. These are described below.

Task 1: Short Passage with Questions

This task has a short passage followed by questions. Read each question carefully. Then write your answer in the space provided.

You can also practice writing skills by completing the Core Writing Skills Practice exercise.

Task 2: Short Passage with Questions

This task has a short passage followed by questions. Read each question carefully. Then write your answer in the space provided.

You can also practice writing skills by completing the Core Writing Skills Practice exercise.

Task 3: Short Story Writing Task

This task requires you to write a short story. Read the writing prompt, complete the planning page, and then write or type your answer.

Task 4: Opinion Piece Writing Task

This final task requires you to write an opinion piece. Read the writing prompt, complete the planning page, and then write or type your answer.

Task 1: Short Passage with Questions

The Zoo

Dear Diary,

Today I went to the zoo again. I saw elephants, monkeys, penguins, and even a lion! But I think my favorite animal is now the alligator. It has dark scaly skin that makes it look a hundred years old and beady eyes that seemed to be staring right at me.

It looked a bit like a dinosaur too. But it was so big and fast. At first I was scared of it. It thrashed around when the zookeeper fed it. It had long white teeth like razors. It snapped its jaws together wildly. Mom told me that it could not climb the fence, so I was not afraid anymore. I knew I would be safe as long as I kept my hands away from the fence.

Until next time,

Fiona

CORE WRITING SKILLS PRACTICE

Describe **two** features that Fiona describes that are shown in the photograph.

_____

_____

_____

_____

1   Why do you think it was important that Fiona kept her hands away from the fence?

Hint   Look for information in the passage that tells you why this would be dangerous. Make sure you use information from the passage in your answer.

_____

_____

_____

_____

_____

2   Describe **two** details given that suggest that the alligator was scary.

1: _____

_____

2: _____

_____

Task 2: Short Passage with Questions

Growing Pains

Spiders belong to the arachnid family. Arachnids are creatures that have no wings, eight legs, and have a body with two parts. Spiders do not have skeletons. Instead, they have a special skin that is known as an exoskeleton. The exoskeleton is hard enough to protect them.

As a spider grows, it needs a larger exoskeleton. Spiders shed their exoskeleton and stretch their bodies until a new exoskeleton forms. Once they stop growing, they do not need to shed their exoskeleton anymore.

CORE WRITING SKILLS PRACTICE
WRITE A RESEARCH REPORT

Choose one of the animals listed below that also has an exoskeleton. Research and write a short report about the animal. Use the questions below to guide your research.

millipede   scorpion   grasshopper   hermit crab

What does the animal look like?

Where does the animal live?

What does the animal eat?

Does the animal replace its exoskeleton? If so, how?

1   Describe what a spider's exoskeleton is.

Hint   Make sure you do not write exactly what is in the passage word for word. Describe what an exoskeleton is in your own words.

_____

_____

_____

_____

_____

2   The chart below gives details about arachnids. Complete the chart using details from the passage.

Feature	Description
Wings	No wings
Number of legs	
Body parts	

Task 3: Short Story Writing Task

Directions: Read the writing prompt below. Use the planning page to plan your writing. Then write or type your answer.

Ken had always loved hiking. He was excited about going hiking in the woods with Uncle Tony.

Write a story about Ken and Uncle Tony's hike.

Hint

The writing prompt tells you that your story should be about a hike. Use this as the starting point and think of a story based around this event.

What happens during the hike is up to you! You could have anything happen during the hike. Maybe Ken and Uncle Tony come across a baby bear or a lost city. Maybe Uncle Tony hurts himself and Ken has to save him. Be creative and try to think of an exciting event that occurs. This will make your story interesting to read.

Planning Page

The Story
Write a summary of your story.

The Beginning
Describe what is going to happen at the start of your story.

The Middle
Describe what is going to happen in the middle of your story.

The End
Describe what is going to happen at the end of your story.

Task 4: Opinion Piece Writing Task

Directions: Read the writing prompt below. Use the planning page to plan your writing. Then write or type your answer.

Some people believe that it is important to have good manners. They think it is important to do things like say please and thank you.

Do you think it is important to have good manners? Why or why not? Use facts, details, or examples to support your opinion.

Hint

You may have several different opinions. You may think that good manners are important. However, you might also think that other things are more important.

A good composition will have one clear idea. Even if you have several ideas, choose one to focus on in your writing. It is better to support one opinion very well than to describe many different opinions!

Planning Page

Summary

Write a brief summary of what you are going to write about.

Supporting Details

Write down the facts, details, or examples you are going to include.

Outline

Write a plan for what you are going to write. Include the main points you want to cover and the order you will cover them.

Writing and Editing Checklist

After you finish writing your opinion piece, you can use this guide to review and edit your work. Use the questions as a guide to finding ways you can improve your work.

Writing Checklist

- ✓ Does your work have one clear opinion?
- ✓ Does your work have a strong opening? Does the opening introduce the topic and state the opinion?
- ✓ Is your opinion supported? Have you used facts, details, and examples to support your opinion?
- ✓ Is your work well-organized? Is related information grouped together? Does each paragraph have one main idea?
- ✓ Do your ideas flow well? Have you used words and phrases to link ideas well?
- ✓ Does your work have a strong ending? Does the ending restate the main idea and tie up the opinion piece?

Editing Checklist

- ✓ Have you used a variety of sentence structures? Are your sentences all written correctly?
- ✓ Is the grammar correct?
- ✓ Are all words spelled correctly? You can check the spelling of any words you are not sure of.
- ✓ Is punctuation used correctly?
- ✓ If dialogue is used, is it punctuated correctly?
- ✓ Are all words capitalized correctly?

Reading and Writing

Practice Set 3

This practice set contains four writing tasks. These are described below.

Task 1: Short Passage with Questions

This task has a short passage followed by questions. Read each question carefully. Then write your answer in the space provided.

You can also practice writing skills by completing the Core Writing Skills Practice exercise.

Task 2: Short Passage with Questions

This task has a short passage followed by questions. Read each question carefully. Then write your answer in the space provided.

You can also practice writing skills by completing the Core Writing Skills Practice exercise.

Task 3: Long Passage with Essay Question

This task has a longer passage with an essay question. Read the passage, complete the planning page, and then write or type your answer.

Task 4: Personal Narrative Writing Task

This final task requires you to write a personal narrative. Read the writing prompt, complete the planning page, and then write or type your answer.

Task 1: Short Passage with Questions

Independence Day

Tom's favorite holiday is Independence Day. However, most people call it the Fourth of July as that is the day it falls on. It is a day that celebrates the United States becoming independent from Great Britain. This happened in 1776.

Tom likes having a big dinner with his family. He also likes inviting his neighbors around. His neighbor Trisha always brings a delicious potato salad. Every year, Keith from across the street brings him a little American flag. Then his neighbor Mr. Bennett plays the piano for everyone. After dinner, everyone has a piece of his mother's cake.

CORE WRITING SKILLS PRACTICE
WRITE A LETTER

Imagine that you are writing to a friend who lives overseas. You want to tell them about Independence Day. You might want to tell them the history of the day, what people do on the day, or what the day means to you. On the lines below, write **three** points you want to make in your letter. Then write your letter.

1. _____

_____

2. _____

_____

3. _____

_____

1   Think about what you do on Independence Day. Describe **one** way that Tom's day and your day are alike.

> **Hint**   This question is asking about your own personal experience. You should compare what you do on Independence Day to what Tom does.

_____

_____

_____

_____

_____

2   Complete the chart below using information from the passage.

People Who Visit Tom	What the Person Does
Trisha	Brings a potato salad
Keith	
Mr. Bennett	

Task 2: Short Passage with Questions

Making Snowflakes

We're going to learn how to use borax to create a crystal snowflake.

Items

Pipe cleaners	String
Heatproof jar	Tablespoon
Borax	Pencil

Directions

1. Use pipe cleaners to create a snowflake shape.
2. Tie a piece of string to one of the edges of your snowflake.
3. Get an adult to pour boiling water into a heatproof jar.
4. Add three tablespoons of borax, one at a time. Mix the solution each time. Make sure the solution is clear before adding the next tablespoon.
5. Tie the string to a pencil. Then put it over the jar so the snowflake shape hangs inside, but does not touch the bottom.
6. Sit the jar overnight. Be sure to not move the jar for 24 hours.
7. Remove the snowflake from the solution and hang wherever you wish.

Remember to be careful when the water is hot!

CORE WRITING SKILLS PRACTICE

Think about how a diagram would be useful in the passage. Describe what a useful diagram would show.

_____

_____

_____

_____

1   What is the main purpose of the passage? Explain your answer.

Hint   Some common purposes are to entertain, to persuade, to instruct or teach, or to explain.

_____

_____

_____

_____

_____

_____

2   Describe what the pencil is used for. Use details from the passage in your answer.

_____

_____

_____

_____

_____

3 Do you think that making a snowflake would be fun? Explain why or why not.

Hint

This question is asking for your personal opinion. Use the information in the passage to decide if making the snowflake sounds fun. Make sure you also explain why you think it would or would not be fun.

_____

_____

_____

_____

_____

_____

_____

_____

_____

_____

_____

_____

Writing and Editing Checklist

After you finish writing your answer to question 3, you can use this guide to review and edit your work. Use the questions as a guide to finding ways you can improve your work.

Writing Checklist

✓ Does your work have one clear opinion?

✓ Does your work have a strong opening? Does the opening introduce the topic and state the opinion?

✓ Is your opinion supported? Have you used facts, details, and examples to support your opinion?

✓ Have you used information from the passage to support your ideas?

✓ Is your work well-organized? Is related information grouped together? Does each paragraph have one main idea?

✓ Do your ideas flow well? Have you used words and phrases to link ideas well?

✓ Does your work have a strong ending? Does the ending restate the main idea and tie up the opinion piece?

Editing Checklist

✓ Have you used a variety of sentence structures? Are your sentences all written correctly?

✓ Is the grammar correct?

✓ Are all words spelled correctly? You can check the spelling of any words you are not sure of.

✓ Is punctuation used correctly?

✓ Are all words capitalized correctly?

Task 3: Long Passage with Essay Question

Directions: Read the passage below. Then answer the question that follows. Use the planning page to plan your writing. Then write or type your essay.

A New Start

Dear Aunt Maria,

What a day! I started at my new school this morning and had the best time. I made lots of new friends and really liked my teachers. I was so nervous the night before, but I had no reason to be. I was really worried that people might be mean to me, or just ignore me. I thought I might feel like an outsider. But everyone was friendly and polite. They made me feel at ease. It was like I'd been at the school for a hundred years!

The day started very early at 7:00 am. I had my breakfast downstairs with my mom. She could tell that I was very anxious. Mom kept asking me what was wrong. I think she knew that I was nervous about starting at a new school. She told me I had nothing to worry about and that everyone was going to love me. If they didn't love me, Mom said to send them her way for a good talking to. I couldn't stop laughing.

My mom dropped me off at the school gates about ten minutes before the bell. A little blonde girl got dropped off at the same time and started waving at me. She ran over and told me her name was Abigail. She was very nice and we became close straight away. We spent all morning together and began to chat to another girl called Stacey. Abigail and Stacey gave me a tour of the school. They showed me where my locker was, and showed me where they usually ate lunch together. They answered a lot of questions I had, and I started to feel a lot more relaxed.

The three of us sat together in class all day and we even made our way home together! Abigail told me that she would introduce me to some other people the next day. She invited me to a party the next week, and asked me if I wanted to join the tennis team with her.

The classes went very quickly as well. Luckily, there wasn't too much work to be done on the first day. I was also relieved that the teacher didn't make me stand in front of the class and introduce myself! That would have been embarrassing. My new teacher gave us a lot of information about what we would learn that year, but that's about it.

It is late now so I am going to sleep, but I cannot wait until tomorrow! I feel as though I am really going to enjoy my time at my new school. I only hope that my new friends feel the same way too.

Casey

1   How is Casey's day different from what she expected? Use details from the passage to support your answer.

In your answer, be sure to
- describe how Casey's day is different from what she expected
- use details from the passage in your answer
- write an answer of between 1 and 2 pages

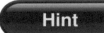

Hint

The key to receiving full marks for this question is to support your answer well.

You can start by writing about what Casey expected the day to be like. Use details from the letter to describe what Casey was worried about.

Then describe how the day actually turned out. Use the details that Casey gives to describe her day.

Finally, end your answer with a conclusion. The conclusion should be a 1-paragraph summary of the main ways her day was different from what she expected.

Planning Page

Summary

Write a brief summary of what you are going to write about.

Supporting Details

Write down the facts, details, or examples you are going to include in your answer.

Outline

Write a plan for what you are going to write. Include the main points you want to cover and the order you will cover them.

Task 4: Personal Narrative Writing Task

Directions: Read the writing prompt below. Use the planning page to plan your writing. Then write or type your answer.

Many people remember times when others were kind to them. Think of a time when somebody was kind to you.

Write a composition describing a time when someone was kind to you. Describe how the person was kind and how it made you feel.

Hint

Stay focused! You might be able to think of many different events you could write about, but don't try to write about them all. Instead, choose just one event and write about that event in detail.

Your answer should describe the event. You should include many details that will help the reader imagine the event. Your answer should also explain how the event made you feel.

Planning Page

Summary

Write a brief summary of what you are going to write about.

Outline

Write a plan for what you are going to write. Include the main points you want to cover and the order you will cover them.

Writing and Editing Checklist

After you finish writing your personal narrative, you can use this guide to review and edit your work. Use the questions as a guide to finding ways you can improve your work.

Writing Checklist

- ✓ Does your work have a strong opening? Does it introduce the main ideas or set the scene well?
- ✓ Is your work well-organized? Is related information grouped together? Does each paragraph have one main idea?
- ✓ Does your work have an effective ending? Does it tie up the events well?
- ✓ Is your work focused? Are there any details that do not fit with your main ideas?
- ✓ Do your ideas flow well? Have you used words and phrases to link ideas well?
- ✓ Have you used strong words? Are there words that could be replaced with better ones?
- ✓ Have you used effective descriptions? Could your descriptions be improved?
- ✓ Have you used sensory details? Could you add more sensory details to help readers imagine the scene?

Editing Checklist

- ✓ Have you used a variety of sentence structures? Are your sentences all written correctly?
- ✓ Is the grammar correct?
- ✓ Are all words spelled correctly? You can check the spelling of any words you are not sure of.
- ✓ Is punctuation used correctly?
- ✓ If dialogue is used, is it punctuated correctly?
- ✓ Are all words capitalized correctly?

Reading and Writing

Practice Set 4

This practice set contains four writing tasks. These are described below.

Task 1: Short Passage with Questions

This task has a short passage followed by questions. Read each question carefully. Then write your answer in the space provided.

You can also practice writing skills by completing the Core Writing Skills Practice exercise.

Task 2: Short Passage with Questions

This task has a short passage followed by questions. Read each question carefully. Then write your answer in the space provided.

You can also practice writing skills by completing the Core Writing Skills Practice exercise.

Task 3: Opinion Piece Writing Task

This task requires you to write an opinion piece. Read the writing prompt, complete the planning page, and then write or type your answer.

Task 4: Short Story Writing Task

This task requires you to write a short story. Read the writing prompt, complete the planning page, and then write or type your answer.

Task 1: Short Passage with Questions

Neptune

Neptune is one of the most interesting planets. It has been studied for many years. Yet scientists still do not know everything about it. Neptune was discovered in 1846 by Heinrich D'Arrest and Johann Galle. There are four gas planets in our Solar System. They are Jupiter, Saturn, Neptune, and Uranus. They are larger than all the other planets. Neptune is the smallest gas planet.

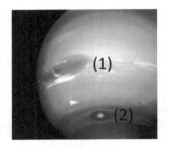

In August 1989, the Voyager spacecraft visited Neptune. It is the only time Neptune has been visited. It was discovered that, like Earth, the sky on Neptune has clouds in it. There are even some storms on Neptune. The storms form what is known as The Great Dark Spot (1) and the Small Dark Spot (2). They are like huge cyclones that form and last for years.

Neptune is the eighth planet from the Sun. It is not as well-known as the largest planet, Jupiter, or Saturn with its rings. It's not easy to study because it's so far away, but scientists are still finding out more about it.

CORE WRITING SKILLS PRACTICE

What is the purpose of the numbers on the photograph of Neptune?

_____

_____

_____

---

1   Describe **three** ways that Neptune is similar to Earth.

> **Hint**   You have to use what you already know about Earth to answer this question. Read each detail given about Neptune. Ask yourself which details are also true about Earth.

1: _____

_____

2: _____

_____

3: _____

_____

2   According to the passage, how is Neptune different from the other gas planets?

_____

_____

_____

_____

_____

_____

Task 2: Short Passage with Questions

Fireworks

The fireworks flew high into the sky. Amazing colors lit up the sky in a sea of purple, green, blue, and orange. The crowd watched as a million rainbows shot out from nowhere.

The crowd was excited to see the amazing display, but Julie was scared. She had never seen a fireworks display and did not like the loud noises. She reached over to her mother and squeezed her hand. Her mother squeezed back and Julie felt a little safer.

CORE WRITING SKILLS PRACTICE

The passage describes the fireworks from a third person point of view. Write a paragraph describing the events from Julie's point of view. Describe what she sees and how she feels.

_____

_____

_____

_____

_____

_____

1   What is the author describing when she says that "a million rainbows shot out from nowhere"?

Hint   The author is not actually describing rainbows. Focus on what the author is trying to help readers imagine.

_____

_____

_____

_____

_____

2   How does Julie feel while watching the fireworks display? Use details from the passage to support your answer.

_____

_____

_____

_____

_____

Task 3: Opinion Piece Writing Task

Directions: Read the writing prompt below. Use the planning page to plan your writing. Then write or type your answer.

Read this proverb about patience.

Good things come to those who wait.

Write an opinion piece for your school newspaper that argues that the proverb is true. In your opinion piece, try to persuade students that it is important to be patient. Use facts, details, or examples in your answer.

Hint

A proverb is a short saying that states an idea. The idea in this proverb is about patience. In your opinion piece, you should tell why this statement is true and why it is important to be patient.

Your answer can be based on your personal experience or on experiences that other students might have. Try to think of examples of how this proverb might relate to students. Use these as examples of why it is important to be patient.

To keep your essay focused, you might like to stay focused on one area. For example, you could write about how students need to be patient when learning new things or how a sportsperson needs to be patient when training and becoming skilled.

Planning Page

Summary

Write a brief summary of what you are going to write about.

Supporting Details

Write down the facts, details, or examples you are going to include.

Outline

Write a plan for what you are going to write. Include the main points you want to cover and the order you will cover them.

Task 4: Short Story Writing Task

Directions: Read the writing prompt below. Use the planning page to plan your writing. Then write or type your answer.

Corey had never baked anything before. But he was happy to try. He had no idea just how many things would go wrong.

Write a story about Corey's baking experience.

Hint

A good story has a beginning, middle, and end. As you plan your story, focus on what is going to happen in each part.

The beginning often introduces the characters and the setting. The start of this story might describe how Corey starts baking.

The middle of the story is where you will describe what goes wrong. This will be the main part of your story. It will usually be 2 or 3 paragraphs long. In this part, describe the events that take place.

At the end of the story, the problem is usually solved. This ties up the story and makes it a complete story.

Planning Page

The Story
Write a summary of your story.

The Beginning
Describe what is going to happen at the start of your story.

The Middle
Describe what is going to happen in the middle of your story.

The End
Describe what is going to happen at the end of your story.

Writing and Editing Checklist

After you finish writing your story, you can use this guide to review and edit your work. Use the questions as a guide to finding ways you can improve your work.

Writing Checklist

- ✓ Does your story have a strong opening? Does it introduce the characters, the setting, or events well?
- ✓ Is your story well-organized? Do the events flow well?
- ✓ Does your story have an effective ending? Does it tie up the story well?
- ✓ Does your story include dialogue? If not, could dialogue make your story better?
- ✓ Have you used strong words? Are there words that could be replaced with better ones?
- ✓ Have you used effective descriptions? Could your descriptions be improved?
- ✓ Have you used sensory details? Could you add more sensory details to help readers imagine the scene?

Editing Checklist

- ✓ Have you used a variety of sentence structures? Are your sentences all written correctly?
- ✓ Is the grammar correct?
- ✓ Are all words spelled correctly? You can check the spelling of any words you are not sure of.
- ✓ Is punctuation used correctly?
- ✓ If dialogue is used, is it punctuated correctly?
- ✓ Are all words capitalized correctly?

Reading and Writing

Practice Set 5

This practice set contains four writing tasks. These are described below.

Task 1: Short Passage with Questions

This task has a short passage followed by questions. Read each question carefully. Then write your answer in the space provided.

You can also practice writing skills by completing the Core Writing Skills Practice exercise.

Task 2: Short Passage with Questions

This task has a short passage followed by questions. Read each question carefully. Then write your answer in the space provided.

You can also practice writing skills by completing the Core Writing Skills Practice exercise.

Task 3: Long Passage with Essay Question

This task has a longer passage with an essay question. Read the passage, complete the planning page, and then write or type your answer.

Task 4: Personal Narrative Writing Task

This final task requires you to write a personal narrative. Read the writing prompt, complete the planning page, and then write or type your answer.

Task 1: Short Passage with Questions

Plastics

Every year 24% of plastics are recycled. This is a lower rate than newspapers. About 80% of newspapers are recycled. About 70% of fiberboard is recycled too.

One of the reasons that plastic is not recycled as often is that it is harder to recycle. There are many different types of plastic. They must be sorted before they can be recycled. Another issue is that many plastics have different colors used in them. This makes them harder to recycle.

It is still encouraged to place plastics in the recycle bin anyway. They will be sorted at recycling plants by workers. Then new items can be made with the old plastic.

CORE WRITING SKILLS PRACTICE
WRITE AN OPINION PIECE

Do you think it is more important to recycle more rubbish or to create less rubbish? List **three** reasons you feel that way. Then write a letter to a newspaper that states your opinion.

1. _____

_____

2. _____

_____

3. _____

_____

1 The chart below shows how much of each type of material is recycled each year. Use details from the passage to complete the chart. Then explain what this shows about how much plastic is recycled.

Item	Amount Recycled Each Year
Plastics	24%
Newspapers	
Fiberboard	

_____

_____

_____

2 Describe **two** reasons that it is difficult to recycle plastics.

1: _____

_____

2: _____

_____

Task 2: Short Passage with Questions

Australia

Australia is not only a country, but it is also a continent. In 1851, gold was discovered in Australia. This led to many people traveling there from all over the world. By 1859, there were six colonies. In 1901, they formed one nation.

Australia now has 8 states and territories. They are Queensland, New South Wales, Northern Territory, South Australia, Victoria, Australian Capital Territory, Western Australia, and Tasmania. New South Wales has the largest population. It also has the largest city, which is Sydney. The capital of Australia is Canberra. It is in the Australian Capital Territory.

State or Territory	Number of People
New South Wales (NSW)	7,200,000
Victoria (VIC)	5,500,000
Queensland (QLD)	4,500,000
Western Australia (WA)	2,300,000
South Australia (SA)	1,600,000
Tasmania (TAS)	510,000
Australian Capital Territory (ACT)	360,000
Northern Territory (NT)	230,000

CORE WRITING SKILLS PRACTICE

Use the map to answer the questions below.

Which state or territory has the largest area? _____

Which state or territory has the smallest area? _____

Which state or territory is an island? _____

In which state or territory is the most northern point? _____

1   How did the discovery of gold affect Australia? Use details from the passage in your answer.

Hint   Be sure to use details from the passage in your answer. But make sure you describe the effect in your own words.

_____

_____

_____

_____

_____

2   Use details from the passage to compare New South Wales (NSW) and the Australian Capital Territory (ACT). Include **two** differences in your answer.

_____

_____

_____

_____

_____

Task 3: Long Passage with Essay Question

Directions: Read the passage below. Then answer the question that follows. Use the planning page to plan your writing. Then write or type your essay.

Gemma's Secret

Nobody knew that Gemma had a secret. Not even her older sister or her parents had the slightest idea. She had never told anyone, as she didn't think that they would understand. Everyone knew that Gemma was creative and imaginative. They also knew that she was a very shy and quiet young girl. What they didn't know is that Gemma's best friend was imaginary. They had been friends for more than two years. Her name was Taylor and she was the very best friend that a young girl could hope for.

Gemma and Taylor would often play together. Taylor followed Gemma like a shadow. They would chase each other in the park. They also liked to play with Gemma's collection of dolls in the back garden.

At night they whispered to each other and shared stories until Gemma drifted off to sleep. Even when Gemma was in the company of other friends, she would always think about Taylor. They were always together and sharing jokes between themselves.

One day Taylor just disappeared. Gemma was very upset that her friend was not around anymore. She looked everywhere for her, but she was nowhere to be found. She couldn't even tell her family why she was so sad because they had no idea Taylor existed.

For a while, Gemma was very quiet and didn't speak very much to anyone. It was only over time that she came to terms with her loss. She made new friends and grew even closer to her sisters.

Losing Taylor made Gemma appreciate her family and loved ones even more. She always remembered Taylor though and all the fun that she brought into her life.

1 Do you think that Gemma having an imaginary friend was good for her? Explain why or why not.

In your answer, be sure to
- give your opinion on whether or not having an imaginary friend was good for Gemma
- explain why you believe this
- use details from the passage in your answer
- write an answer of between 1 and 2 pages

This question is asking for your personal opinion. You can decide for yourself whether or not you think the imaginary friend was a good thing. You will not be marked based on which opinion you hold. Instead, you will be marked on how well you explain your opinion and support it with details from the passage.

To start, first decide whether you think the imaginary friend was good for her or not. Then think of 2 or 3 reasons why you think this. In your answer, you should clearly describe these reasons. For each reason, you should use details from the passage.

Planning Page

Summary

Write a brief summary of what you are going to write about.

Supporting Details

Write down the facts, details, or examples you are going to include in your answer.

Outline

Write a plan for what you are going to write. Include the main points you want to cover and the order you will cover them.

Task 4: Personal Narrative Writing Task

Directions: Read the writing prompt below. Use the planning page to plan your writing. Then write or type your answer.

Mother Knows Best

I wanted to eat my dinner in bed.
My mother said, "Eat at the table instead!"
I did not listen. I should have thought twice.
Now my bedroom is home to two hungry mice!

The poet describes a time when he did not listen to his mother when he should have. Write a composition about a time when you didn't listen to someone. Describe what happened because you didn't listen and what you learned from it.

Hint

This writing task introduces the topic by using a poem. You do not have to refer to the poem in your answer. The poem is just there to help you start thinking about the topic.

The goal of your writing is to write about a time when you didn't listen to someone. You should also clearly describe what happened because you didn't listen and what you learned.

Planning Page

Summary

Write a brief summary of what you are going to write about.

Outline

Write a plan for what you are going to write. Include the main points you want to cover and the order you will cover them.

Writing and Editing Checklist

After you finish writing your personal narrative, you can use this guide to review and edit your work. Use the questions as a guide to finding ways you can improve your work.

Writing Checklist

- ✓ Does your work have a strong opening? Does it introduce the main ideas or set the scene well?
- ✓ Is your work well-organized? Is related information grouped together? Does each paragraph have one main idea?
- ✓ Does your work have an effective ending? Does it tie up the events well?
- ✓ Is your work focused? Are there any details that do not fit with your main ideas?
- ✓ Do your ideas flow well? Have you used words and phrases to link ideas well?
- ✓ Have you used strong words? Are there words that could be replaced with better ones?
- ✓ Have you used effective descriptions? Could your descriptions be improved?
- ✓ Have you used sensory details? Could you add more sensory details to help readers imagine the scene?

Editing Checklist

- ✓ Have you used a variety of sentence structures? Are your sentences all written correctly?
- ✓ Is the grammar correct?
- ✓ Are all words spelled correctly? You can check the spelling of any words you are not sure of.
- ✓ Is punctuation used correctly?
- ✓ If dialogue is used, is it punctuated correctly?
- ✓ Are all words capitalized correctly?

Reading and Writing

Practice Set 6

This practice set contains four writing tasks. These are described below.

Task 1: Short Passage with Questions

This task has a short passage followed by questions. Read each question carefully. Then write your answer in the space provided.

You can also practice writing skills by completing the Core Writing Skills Practice exercise.

Task 2: Short Passage with Questions

This task has a short passage followed by questions. Read each question carefully. Then write your answer in the space provided.

You can also practice writing skills by completing the Core Writing Skills Practice exercise.

Task 3: Short Story Writing Task

This task requires you to write a short story. Read the writing prompt, complete the planning page, and then write or type your answer.

Task 4: Opinion Piece Writing Task

This final task requires you to write an opinion piece. Read the writing prompt, complete the planning page, and then write or type your answer.

Task 1: Short Passage with Questions

A Tasty Trick

My dad has always said that I have to eat vegetables for my body to stay healthy. I never used to like vegetables much. In fact, I kept saying that all vegetables taste horrible. He'd pile carrots on my plate, but I'd push them off to the side. He'd tell me peas were delicious, but I wouldn't even try one little pea. Dad got annoyed that I wouldn't try different things. He was also worried that I would end up sick. So Dad decided to try something new to make sure I would eat them. He came up with a little plan.

He started putting vegetables in dishes like spaghetti or inside meat pies. He'd grate them or blend them so I wouldn't even see them. That way, I didn't even know I was eating vegetables. The funny thing was that I actually liked the taste. Now I no longer avoid vegetables. I am happy to eat them however they are served.

CORE WRITING SKILLS PRACTICE

What details in the passage suggest that the father did the right thing by coming up with a plan to get the narrator to eat vegetables? Explain.

_____

_____

_____

_____

_____

_____

---

1   Describe why "A Tasty Trick" is a good title for the passage.

Hint   Focus on why this title suits what the passage is about.

_____

_____

_____

_____

_____

2   How did the narrator's father get her to eat vegetables?

_____

_____

_____

_____

_____

Task 2: Short Passage with Questions

Recycle Today

Recycling is really important. You can recycle glass, plastic, and paper. You put your trash made out of these materials into a special recycling bin. Then it is sorted by workers. After it is sorted, it is cleaned. Then it is made into new materials. In the end, your trash is turned into new items!

Recycling helps to save the environment. It helps because new glass, paper, and plastic doesn't need to be created. You should do your part and recycle! If everyone recycled, the world would be a better place.

Look out for recycling bins. Make sure you place material that can be recycled in them.

CORE WRITING SKILLS PRACTICE

The author states that the world would be a better place if everyone recycled. Do you agree with this statement? Explain why or why not.

_____

_____

_____

_____

_____

1   The diagram shows how materials are recycled. Complete the missing steps in the diagram.

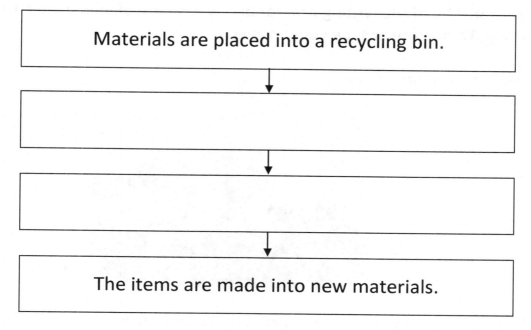

Materials are placed into a recycling bin.

The items are made into new materials.

2   Do you think the main purpose of the passage is to inform or persuade? Use details from the passage to support your answer.

Hint   A passage that informs wants to tell you facts. One that persuades wants to get you to do something.

_____

_____

_____

_____

_____

Task 3: Short Story Writing Task

Directions: Read the writing prompt below. Use the planning page to plan your writing. Then write or type your answer.

Look at the picture below.

Write a story based on what is happening in the picture.

Your story should be based on the picture given. You should use the picture to come up with an idea for your story.

The story shows students next to a swimming pool. The students are cheering for someone. Think about why the race is so important or why it means so much to everyone. Use this to come up with an idea. Your main character could be somebody cheering or the person they are cheering for. Make sure you come up with a complete story based on the picture.

Planning Page

The Story
Write a summary of your story.

The Beginning
Describe what is going to happen at the start of your story.

The Middle
Describe what is going to happen in the middle of your story.

The End
Describe what is going to happen at the end of your story.

Task 4: Opinion Piece Writing Task

Directions: Read the writing prompt below. Use the planning page to plan your writing. Then write or type your answer.

Read this proverb about giving.

It is better to give than to receive.

Do you agree with this proverb? Explain why or why not. Use facts, details, or examples in your answer.

Hint

A proverb is a short saying that states an idea. The idea in this proverb is that giving to others is better than receiving. You have to explain whether or not you agree with this.

When you are asked whether or not you agree with something, you will not be scored based on whether you agree or not. You will be scored on how well you explain why you do or do not agree. Don't worry about choosing the right answer. Instead, focus on what your personal opinion is. Then focus on clearly explaining why this is your opinion.

Planning Page

Summary

Write a brief summary of what you are going to write about.

Supporting Details

Write down the facts, details, or examples you are going to include.

Outline

Write a plan for what you are going to write. Include the main points you want to cover and the order you will cover them.

Writing and Editing Checklist

After you finish writing your opinion piece, you can use this guide to review and edit your work. Use the questions as a guide to finding ways you can improve your work.

Writing Checklist

- ✓ Does your work have one clear opinion?
- ✓ Does your work have a strong opening? Does the opening introduce the topic and state the opinion?
- ✓ Is your opinion supported? Have you used facts, details, and examples to support your opinion?
- ✓ Is your work well-organized? Is related information grouped together? Does each paragraph have one main idea?
- ✓ Do your ideas flow well? Have you used words and phrases to link ideas well?
- ✓ Does your work have a strong ending? Does the ending restate the main idea and tie up the opinion piece?

Editing Checklist

- ✓ Have you used a variety of sentence structures? Are your sentences all written correctly?
- ✓ Is the grammar correct?
- ✓ Are all words spelled correctly? You can check the spelling of any words you are not sure of.
- ✓ Is punctuation used correctly?
- ✓ If dialogue is used, is it punctuated correctly?
- ✓ Are all words capitalized correctly?

Reading and Writing

Practice Set 7

This practice set contains four writing tasks. These are described below.

Task 1: Short Passage with Questions

This task has a short passage followed by questions. Read each question carefully. Then write your answer in the space provided.

You can also practice writing skills by completing the Core Writing Skills Practice exercise.

Task 2: Short Passage with Questions

This task has a short passage followed by questions. Read each question carefully. Then write your answer in the space provided.

You can also practice writing skills by completing the Core Writing Skills Practice exercise.

Task 3: Long Passage with Essay Question

This task has a longer passage with an essay question. Read the passage, complete the planning page, and then write or type your answer.

Task 4: Explanatory Writing Task

This final task requires you to write an essay that explains something. Read the writing prompt, complete the planning page, and then write or type your answer.

Task 1: Short Passage with Questions

View from the Moon

Many people believe that the Great Wall of China can be viewed from the Moon. This is actually incorrect. No manmade structures are visible from the Moon at all. Continents, oceans, and cloud cover can be seen. But structures like buildings cannot be seen.

It is true that the Great Wall of China can be viewed from space. But so can many other structures. These include motorways, cities, landmarks, and even fields of crops.

The Great Wall of China is an amazing thing to see. It is just over 13,000 miles long. It was first built thousands of years ago. However, it is a myth that the wall can be seen from the Moon.

©Severin Stalder, Wikimedia Commons

CORE WRITING SKILLS PRACTICE

Many tourists visit The Great Wall of China each year. What do you think makes people want to visit the landmark?

_____

_____

_____

_____

1   What is the main idea of the passage?

Hint   In your answer, describe what the author wants readers of the passage to learn from it.

_____

_____

_____

_____

_____

_____

2   List the items that can be seen from the Moon. List the items that can be seen from space.

Moon: _____

_____

Space: _____

_____

Task 2: Short Passage with Questions

Comets

Comets are balls of dust or ice that move through the atmosphere. They come from two different places in space. One is known as the Kuiper Belt. The other is known as the Oort Cloud.

Both of those locations are orbiting the Sun. But they are far from the Sun. The Kuiper Belt is just past Neptune. The Oort Cloud is much farther away. It is far out past even Pluto.

They are so far away that the ice making up the comets does not melt. However, sometimes comets do come closer to the Sun. Then the ice begins to melt. This leaves a trail behind them. This gives comets their unique appearance.

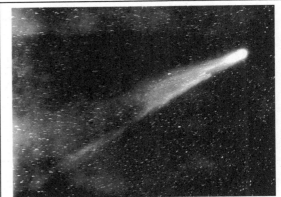

When comets are viewed from Earth, they often look like they have a tail behind them.

CORE WRITING SKILLS PRACTICE
WRITE A RESEARCH REPORT

One of the most well-known comets is named Halley's Comet. It is well-known because it can be viewed from Earth. Research and write a short report about Halley's Comet. Use the questions below to guide your research.

When was Halley's Comet first discovered?

Who discovered Halley's Comet?

When is Halley's Comet able to be seen from Earth?

What does Halley's Comet look like when viewed from Earth?

1   Why do comets that come close to the Sun appear to have a tail? Explain
       your answer.

_____

_____

_____

_____

_____

_____

2   Describe the **two** places that comets come from.

Hint   Make sure you do not just name each place. You should also
                  describe where each place is.

1: _____

_____

2: _____

_____

Task 3: Long Passage with Essay Question

Directions: Read the passage below. Then answer the question that follows. Use the planning page to plan your writing. Then write or type your essay.

Trying Too Hard

Robert was determined to do well in his exams. He devoted all of his spare time to study. He had always wanted to be a lawyer when he grew up. He wanted to go to a good college and enjoy a successful career. Unfortunately, this meant that he was almost always serious.

Even though he was young, he was unable to relax and enjoy himself most of the time. His friends often got frustrated that he didn't want to spend much time with them.

Robert had an important exam due the following day. He had spent almost an entire week preparing for it. He had managed to get little sleep and was very tired. He even spent the night before the exam revising and had barely managed any sleep at all. However, he thought that he was ready for the exam. He was confident that he had worked harder than anyone else and was sure to get a perfect grade.

After Robert ate his breakfast, he started to feel a little ill. He was tired and unable to focus. He also had a small headache and found it very difficult to concentrate. He still refused to believe that he could ever fail the exam. Robert arrived at the school hall and took his seat beside his friends. He noticed how relaxed and happy they looked compared to him.

"They are just underprepared," he thought to himself as he began his paper.

Despite his best efforts, Robert wasn't able to finish his exam. After twenty minutes, he felt very hot and uncomfortable. He then slumped in his chair, and one of his friends called for help. The school doctor suggested that he was exhausted and would be unable to complete the exam.

He spent the lunch break in the nurse's office. He looked out the window and watched his friends. They smiled and joked and seemed to have not a care in the world. Robert decided that from then on, he wouldn't take it all so seriously.

"I guess I will know better next time," he mumbled.

1   The passage describes a boy who takes things too seriously. Think of a time when you took something too seriously. Describe that time and how it is similar to Robert's experience.

In your answer, be sure to

- describe a time when you took something too seriously
- describe how your situation was similar to Robert's experience
- use details from the passage in your answer
- write an answer of between 1 and 2 pages

Hint

The question asks you to relate to the passage. You have to write about your own experience of taking something too seriously.

You will mainly use your own experience in your essay. You should describe what you took seriously and what happened. Be sure to provide enough details so the reader knows what happened.

Then relate your experience to Robert's. You might describe how you both learned not to be so serious, or how things worked out poorly for you just like they did for Robert.

Planning Page

Summary

Write a brief summary of what you are going to write about.

Supporting Details

Write down the facts, details, or examples you are going to include in your answer.

Outline

Write a plan for what you are going to write. Include the main points you want to cover and the order you will cover them.

Task 4: Explanatory Writing Task

Directions: Read the writing prompt below. Use the planning page to plan your writing. Then write or type your answer.

Some people enjoy summer weather the most. They might enjoy going to the beach or lazing by the pool. Other people like winter weather the most. They might enjoy relaxing by a warm fire or playing in the snow.

Write a composition describing whether you like summer or winter weather the most. Explain why you like that type of weather the most.

Hint

When writing compositions like this, you should focus on 2 or 3 things that you like most. There may be many more things that you like. However, it is better to describe 2 or 3 things in detail than to list many things you like.

You will be scored on how well you describe what you like, not on how many things you can think of! When you write your plan, choose the 2 or 3 things you like most and write one paragraph about each thing.

Planning Page

Summary

Write a brief summary of what you are going to write about.

Supporting Details

Write down the facts, details, or examples you are going to include.

Outline

Write a plan for what you are going to write. Include the main points you want to cover and the order you will cover them.

Writing and Editing Checklist

After you finish writing your essay, you can use this guide to review and edit your work. Use the questions as a guide to finding ways you can improve your work.

Writing Checklist

- ✓ Does your work have a strong opening? Does it introduce the topic and the main ideas?
- ✓ Is your work well-organized? Is related information grouped together? Does each paragraph have one main idea?
- ✓ Have you included facts, details, and examples to support your ideas?
- ✓ Is your work focused? Are there any details that do not fit with your main ideas?
- ✓ Do your ideas flow well? Have you used words and phrases to link ideas well?
- ✓ Does your work have a strong ending?

Editing Checklist

- ✓ Have you used a variety of sentence structures? Are your sentences all written correctly?
- ✓ Is the grammar correct?
- ✓ Are all words spelled correctly? You can check the spelling of any words you are not sure of.
- ✓ Is punctuation used correctly?
- ✓ Are all words capitalized correctly?

Reading and Writing

Practice Set 8

This practice set contains four writing tasks. These are described below.

Task 1: Short Passage with Questions

This task has a short passage followed by questions. Read each question carefully. Then write your answer in the space provided.

You can also practice writing skills by completing the Core Writing Skills Practice exercise.

Task 2: Short Passage with Questions

This task has a short passage followed by questions. Read each question carefully. Then write your answer in the space provided.

You can also practice writing skills by completing the Core Writing Skills Practice exercise.

Task 3: Opinion Piece Writing Task

This task requires you to write an opinion piece. Read the writing prompt, complete the planning page, and then write or type your answer.

Task 4: Short Story Writing Task

This task requires you to write a short story. Read the writing prompt, complete the planning page, and then write or type your answer.

Task 1: Short Passage with Questions

Better Than Expected

Rat was hiding in her little hole in the wall. She was curled up, playing with her whiskers. She heard the human family that lived in the house close the front door. This was her favorite time! She scurried around the human's kitchen finding tasty snacks. Then she saw Cat. She was so scared that she froze. Cat purred quietly and walked over to her. Rat was so frightened that she couldn't even move. Her legs began to shake.

"Don't be scared Rat," Cat said. "Jump on my back and I can get you to the counter where the cheese is!"

Rat jumped on her back and crawled up to the kitchen bench. Cat jumped up after her. They feasted together and agreed to meet again the next time the humans left.

CORE WRITING SKILLS PRACTICE

What lesson does the story have about judging others right away? In your answer, describe how Rat judges Cat but is wrong about her.

_____

_____

_____

_____

_____

_____

---

1   Explain why the end of the passage is a surprise.

Hint   Focus on how what you expect to happen is different from what does happen.

_____

_____

_____

_____

_____

2   How can you tell that the events in the passage could not really happen?

Hint   The events in the passage are made-up and could not happen in real life. Explain how you can tell this.

_____

_____

_____

_____

Task 2: Short Passage with Questions

Rookie

Today was my first day of basketball practice. We had to wear shirts that have numbers and our names on the back. One of the first things I learned is that bouncing the ball is called dribbling. When the coach first told us, I couldn't stop laughing about it! The coach told me to stop laughing. He said I should take basketball more seriously.

Most of the lesson was spent trying to throw the ball up and into the hoop. At first, the balls were going everywhere. It was as if the basketballs had minds of their own. We learned that you can bounce the ball off the backboard. When it goes through the hoop, it's called getting a basket. I scored three baskets! I am excited for when I will be good enough to play my first game.

CORE WRITING SKILLS PRACTICE

The passage describes a person learning a new sport. Think of a time when you learned to do something new. Was it fun or difficult? Write a few paragraphs describing that time.

_____

_____

_____

_____

_____

_____

_____

1   Explain why the narrator is told to take basketball more seriously.

Hint   This is a cause and effect question. Focus on what the narrator did that made the coach say this.

_____

_____

_____

_____

_____

2   The narrator says that it was "as if the basketballs had minds of their own." What does the narrator mean by this?

_____

_____

_____

_____

_____

3   Do you think the narrator enjoyed basketball practice? Explain why or why not. Use details from the passage to support your answer.

Hint

Start your answer by giving your opinion on whether or not the narrator enjoyed basketball practice. Then explain why you think that. Use details from the passage when you explain why you think that.

_____

_____

_____

_____

_____

_____

_____

_____

_____

_____

_____

Writing and Editing Checklist

After you finish writing your answer to question 3, you can use this guide to review and edit your work. Use the questions as a guide to finding ways you can improve your work.

Writing Checklist

- ✓ Does your work have one clear opinion?
- ✓ Does your work have a strong opening? Does the opening introduce the topic and state the opinion?
- ✓ Is your opinion supported? Have you used facts, details, and examples to support your opinion?
- ✓ Have you used information from the passage to support your ideas?
- ✓ Is your work well-organized? Is related information grouped together? Does each paragraph have one main idea?
- ✓ Do your ideas flow well? Have you used words and phrases to link ideas well?
- ✓ Does your work have a strong ending? Does the ending restate the main idea and tie up the opinion piece?

Editing Checklist

- ✓ Have you used a variety of sentence structures? Are your sentences all written correctly?
- ✓ Is the grammar correct?
- ✓ Are all words spelled correctly? You can check the spelling of any words you are not sure of.
- ✓ Is punctuation used correctly?
- ✓ Are all words capitalized correctly?

Task 3: Opinion Piece Writing Task

Directions: Read the writing prompt below. Use the planning page to plan your writing. Then write or type your answer.

Think about the place where you live. Do you think it is a good place to live? Write an essay that gives your opinion on the place you live. Use facts, details, or examples to support your opinion.

Hint

When completing these writing tasks, it is important to include supporting details. In some tasks, you can use facts. In a task like this, it is often better to use details and examples.

Once you have decided whether or not where you live is a good place to live, think of details and examples you can use to support your opinion. For example, if you live in a small town, you might describe how you know a lot of people. You could give an example of people from the town helping each other out.

Planning Page

Summary
Write a brief summary of what you are going to write about.

Supporting Details
Write down the facts, details, or examples you are going to include.

Outline
Write a plan for what you are going to write. Include the main points you want to cover and the order you will cover them.

Task 4: Short Story Writing Task

Directions: Read the writing prompt below. Use the planning page to plan your writing. Then write or type your answer.

Look at the picture below.

Write a story based on what is happening in the picture.

One way to write a good story is to choose a style of writing and stick to it. The picture could be the start of a funny story. It could also be the start of an adventure story. As you think of an idea for your story, also think about what type of story you want to write.

Planning Page

The Story
Write a summary of your story.

The Beginning
Describe what is going to happen at the start of your story.

The Middle
Describe what is going to happen in the middle of your story.

The End
Describe what is going to happen at the end of your story.

Writing and Editing Checklist

After you finish writing your story, you can use this guide to review and edit your work. Use the questions as a guide to finding ways you can improve your work.

Writing Checklist

✓ Does your story have a strong opening? Does it introduce the characters, the setting, or events well?

✓ Is your story well-organized? Do the events flow well?

✓ Does your story have an effective ending? Does it tie up the story well?

✓ Does your story include dialogue? If not, could dialogue make your story better?

✓ Have you used strong words? Are there words that could be replaced with better ones?

✓ Have you used effective descriptions? Could your descriptions be improved?

✓ Have you used sensory details? Could you add more sensory details to help readers imagine the scene?

Editing Checklist

✓ Have you used a variety of sentence structures? Are your sentences all written correctly?

✓ Is the grammar correct?

✓ Are all words spelled correctly? You can check the spelling of any words you are not sure of.

✓ Is punctuation used correctly?

✓ If dialogue is used, is it punctuated correctly?

✓ Are all words capitalized correctly?

Reading and Writing

Practice Set 9

This practice set contains four writing tasks. These are described below.

Task 1: Short Passage with Questions

This task has a short passage followed by questions. Read each question carefully. Then write your answer in the space provided.

You can also practice writing skills by completing the Core Writing Skills Practice exercise.

Task 2: Short Passage with Questions

This task has a short passage followed by questions. Read each question carefully. Then write your answer in the space provided.

You can also practice writing skills by completing the Core Writing Skills Practice exercise.

Task 3: Long Passage with Essay Question

This task has a longer passage with an essay question. Read the passage, complete the planning page, and then write or type your answer.

Task 4: Explanatory Writing Task

This final task requires you to write an essay that explains something. Read the writing prompt, complete the planning page, and then write or type your answer.

Task 1: Short Passage with Questions

Take a Deep Breath

The lung is an organ that is used to help many living things breathe. Humans have two lungs in their body. The lungs have several important purposes. The main purpose of the lungs is to take in oxygen from the air. Carbon dioxide leaves the body via the lungs. The lungs are also used to protect the heart from any sudden shocks to the chest. Another purpose of the lungs is to filter blood clots.

Healthy Lungs

It is important to take good care of your lungs. One of the best ways to keep your lungs healthy is to exercise often. This gives your lungs a workout! The more you exercise, the stronger your lungs will become!

CORE WRITING SKILLS PRACTICE

The heart and the lungs work together to take oxygen to the cells of the body. Use the Internet to find out information about the heart. Then describe how the heart and the lungs work together.

_____

_____

_____

_____

_____

1   What is the main purpose of the information in the box?

Hint   Make sure you only describe the purpose of the information in the box titled "Healthy Lungs," and not the purpose of the whole passage.

_____

_____

_____

_____

_____

_____

2   Describe **three** different purposes of the lungs.

1: _____

_____

2: _____

_____

3: _____

_____

Task 2: Short Passage with Questions

Making a Peg Doll

We are going to make a fun and cheap toy called a peg doll using wooden clothes pins. It's easy to make a clothes pin into a doll because it's already shaped like one! Here is how you do it:

1. Start by getting a wooden clothes pin.

2. Use a marker to draw a face on the round end of the clothes pin.

3. Wrap a pipe cleaner around the center of the peg to give your doll arms.

4. Cut out a rectangle of fabric to glue onto the doll for clothes.

5. Cut five pieces of wool and glue them to the head for the doll's hair.

CORE WRITING SKILLS PRACTICE

The author states that a clothes pin is already shaped like a doll. Use the picture below to help explain this statement. You could label the clothes pin or describe how they are like dolls in words.

---

1   Using the information from the passage, complete the list below of the items needed to make a peg doll.

Items Needed to Make a Peg Doll
1. Clothes pin
2.
3.
4.
5.
6. Glue

2   Would you like to make a peg doll? Explain why or why not.

_____

_____

_____

_____

_____

Task 3: Long Passage with Essay Question

Directions: Read the passage below. Then answer the question that follows. Use the planning page to plan your writing. Then write or type your essay.

Happy Campers Summer Retreat

As a parent, your child's happiness is the most important thing to you. It is important to keep children healthy and active. This can be difficult to achieve. After all, many people have busy careers as well. The Happy Campers Summer Retreat was developed to help parents with this challenge.

Michael Gibson founded our group in 1998. We run a summer camp for children during the holidays. We are open from May to September. We look after lots of children every single year. The camp is based in the Colorado Mountains. It offers a wide range of activities for children. Our group's mission is to create a new generation of active children across America.

Our program helps improve:
- Physical fitness
- Problem-solving skills
- Social skills
- Sports ability and experience

The Happy Campers Summer Retreat can benefit all children. Some children are good at school, but rarely active. Our program will help encourage an interest in sports. Other children are mainly interested in sports. These children will play sports, but will also learn new skills. Team sports are also very important. They are used to help children develop teamwork skills, social skills, and communication skills. Children will also have the chance to try new activities. Our program is designed to help develop a complete and fully active child.

Our program is very affordable. It is available to any family in America. Your child's stay can be as short as a week or as long as six weeks. We will also cater to any special needs that your child may have.

Why not call us today or send us an email with your enquiry? Take action now and give your child this great opportunity! Our helpful staff will be able to give you all of the answers that you need.

1   What are the main benefits of the Happy Campers Summer Retreat? If you attended the retreat, which benefit do you think would be most important to you? Use details from the passage in your answer.

In your answer, be sure to
- describe the main benefits of the Happy Campers Summer Retreat
- describe which benefit would be most important to you
- use details from the passage in your answer
- write an answer of between 1 and 2 pages

Hint

There are two parts to this writing task. You should start by describing what the main benefits of the retreat are. Use the information in the passage to explain what the main benefits are.

You should then write about how one benefit relates to you. Choose one benefit that you think would be most important to you. Write a paragraph or two describing why you choose this benefit or how this benefit would help you personally.

Planning Page

Summary

Write a brief summary of what you are going to write about.

Supporting Details

Write down the facts, details, or examples you are going to include in your answer.

Outline

Write a plan for what you are going to write. Include the main points you want to cover and the order you will cover them.

Task 4: Explanatory Writing Task

Directions: Read the writing prompt below. Use the planning page to plan your writing. Then write or type your answer.

Many people have a special talent. Some people are good at sport. Other people are good at cooking or writing. What special talent do you have?

Write a composition describing a special talent that you have. Explain what you are good at and how you discovered you were good at it.

Hint

When planning your writing, it is a good idea to break down what you want to say into paragraphs. This will help make sure your writing is well-organized and easy to understand. In your outline, describe what you are going to cover in each paragraph. Make sure that each paragraph has one main idea.

Planning Page

Summary

Write a brief summary of what you are going to write about.

Outline

Write a plan for what you are going to write. Include the main points you want to cover and the order you will cover them.

Writing and Editing Checklist

After you finish writing your essay, you can use this guide to review and edit your work. Use the questions as a guide to finding ways you can improve your work.

Writing Checklist

- ✓ Does your work have a strong opening? Does it introduce the topic and the main ideas?
- ✓ Is your work well-organized? Is related information grouped together? Does each paragraph have one main idea?
- ✓ Have you included facts, details, and examples to support your ideas?
- ✓ Is your work focused? Are there any details that do not fit with your main ideas?
- ✓ Do your ideas flow well? Have you used words and phrases to link ideas well?
- ✓ Does your work have a strong ending?

Editing Checklist

- ✓ Have you used a variety of sentence structures? Are your sentences all written correctly?
- ✓ Is the grammar correct?
- ✓ Are all words spelled correctly? You can check the spelling of any words you are not sure of.
- ✓ Is punctuation used correctly?
- ✓ Are all words capitalized correctly?

Reading and Writing

Practice Set 10

This practice set contains four writing tasks. These are described below.

Task 1: Short Passage with Questions

This task has a short passage followed by questions. Read each question carefully. Then write your answer in the space provided.

You can also practice writing skills by completing the Core Writing Skills Practice exercise.

Task 2: Short Passage with Questions

This task has a short passage followed by questions. Read each question carefully. Then write your answer in the space provided.

You can also practice writing skills by completing the Core Writing Skills Practice exercise.

Task 3: Short Story Writing Task

This task requires you to write a short story. Read the writing prompt, complete the planning page, and then write or type your answer.

Task 4: Opinion Piece Writing Task

This final task requires you to write an opinion piece. Read the writing prompt, complete the planning page, and then write or type your answer.

Task 1: Short Passage with Questions

Pizza Night

Dear Grandpa,

Tonight we had pizza for dinner. My favorite food is pizza. Dad likes pepperoni pizza the most and Mom likes cheese pizza best. My favorite is ham and pineapple. What is your favorite type of pizza? Dad thinks people are strange for putting pineapple on a pizza. But I like the sweet taste. It is absolutely delicious! Another reason I like it is because there is no onion on it. I hate onion! It seems like it comes on all pizzas, but it is never on ham and pineapple pizzas. I hope I have pizza for dinner again soon. Well, I better get going.

Your granddaughter,

Sandy

CORE WRITING SKILLS PRACTICE

What is your favorite food? Explain why you like that food so much.

_____

_____

_____

_____

_____

_____

_____

1   Use information from the passage to complete the table below.

Person	Favorite Type of Pizza
Sandy	Ham and pineapple
Dad	
Mom	

2   Why does Sandy like ham and pineapple pizza?

Hint   Look for details that Sandy gives that show why she likes ham and pineapple pizza.

_____

_____

_____

_____

_____

Task 2: Short Passage with Questions

Friends in Far Places

My name is Dan. I have a pen pal who lives in France. His name is Jean-Luc. He writes me letters and tells me all about his life. We talk about school, our pets, our families, playing sport, and many other things. Even though we live in different countries, we have a lot in common and get along very well.

Last week I sent him an American Flag and a penny in the mail. He sent back a chocolate bar and some stamps from his country. I took them to show and tell at school. All of my classmates were jealous. They asked if Jean-Luc had any friends to be their pen pals!

CORE WRITING SKILLS PRACTICE

Pen pals are people who write letters to each other. Many people do not write letters as much as they used to because it is easier to chat to others using email or the Internet. Think about what makes writing letters special. Write a paragraph in which you argue that writing letters is important.

_____

_____

_____

_____

_____

_____

_____

1   Complete the web below using information from the passage.

Hint — When answering questions like this, make sure you use information that is given in the passage. Only list things mentioned in the passage.

```
┌──────────────┐                    ┌──────────────┐
│              │                    │              │
│              │                    │              │
└──────────────┘                    └──────────────┘
            ┌─────────────────────┐
            │   Things that Dan   │
            │  and Jean-Luc Talk  │
            │       About         │
            └─────────────────────┘
┌──────────────┐                    ┌──────────────┐
│              │                    │              │
│              │                    │              │
└──────────────┘                    └──────────────┘
```

2   Would you like to have a pen pal? Explain why or why not.

_____

_____

_____

_____

_____

Task 3: Short Story Writing Task

Directions: Read the writing prompt below. Use the planning page to plan your writing. Then write or type your answer.

Kendra walked her dog Candy to the park. She did this every afternoon. But this afternoon was going to be different. Something very unusual was about to happen.

Write a story about what happens at the park.

Hint

One way to improve your writing is to focus on how you describe things. You can choose words and phrases that make your writing more interesting.

Imagine that you want to describe how Candy ran off. Instead of saying that Candy ran away, you might say that she raced off like a lion was after her. Instead of saying that Candy barked loudly, you might say that she barked so loudly that the trees shook. By describing things in a more interesting way, you will make your story more interesting to the reader.

Planning Page

The Story

Write a summary of your story.

The Beginning

Describe what is going to happen at the start of your story.

The Middle

Describe what is going to happen in the middle of your story.

The End

Describe what is going to happen at the end of your story.

Task 4: Opinion Piece Writing Task

Directions: Read the writing prompt below. Use the planning page to plan your writing. Then write or type your answer.

Read this piece of advice.

It's no use crying over spilled milk.

Do you think this is good advice? Explain why or why not.

Hint

Start by thinking about what the advice means. It means that there is no point getting upset about something that has happened. Then think about whether you agree. Think about how this advice relates to your life.

A good essay will be focused. Think about how it relates to one area of your life. You might also think of a certain situation where this would have been good advice. As you plan your writing, focus on this one area. This will help make sure you produce writing that has a clear and focused idea.

Planning Page

Summary

Write a brief summary of what you are going to write about.

Supporting Details

Write down the facts, details, or examples you are going to include.

Outline

Write a plan for what you are going to write. Include the main points you want to cover and the order you will cover them.

Writing and Editing Checklist

After you finish writing your opinion piece, you can use this guide to review and edit your work. Use the questions as a guide to finding ways you can improve your work.

Writing Checklist

- ✓ Does your work have one clear opinion?
- ✓ Does your work have a strong opening? Does the opening introduce the topic and state the opinion?
- ✓ Is your opinion supported? Have you used facts, details, and examples to support your opinion?
- ✓ Is your work well-organized? Is related information grouped together? Does each paragraph have one main idea?
- ✓ Do your ideas flow well? Have you used words and phrases to link ideas well?
- ✓ Does your work have a strong ending? Does the ending restate the main idea and tie up the opinion piece?

Editing Checklist

- ✓ Have you used a variety of sentence structures? Are your sentences all written correctly?
- ✓ Is the grammar correct?
- ✓ Are all words spelled correctly? You can check the spelling of any words you are not sure of.
- ✓ Is punctuation used correctly?
- ✓ Are all words capitalized correctly?

Answer Key

Developing Common Core Reading and Writing Skills

The state of Washington has adopted the Common Core State Standards. Student learning throughout the year is based on these standards, and all the questions on the state tests assess these standards. All the questions and exercises in this workbook are based on the knowledge and skills described in the Common Core State Standards. While this workbook focuses specifically on the Common Core writing standards, the questions based on passages also assess Common Core reading standards.

Core Skills Practice Exercises

Each short passage in this workbook includes an exercise focused on one key skill described in the Common Core standards. The answer key identifies the core skill covered by each exercise, and describes what to look for in the student's response.

Scoring Constructed-Response Questions

The short passages in this workbook include constructed-response questions, where students provide a written answer to a question. Short questions are scored out of 2 and longer questions are scored out of 4. The answer key gives guidance on how to score these questions. Use the criteria listed as a guide to scoring these questions, and as a guide for giving the student advice on how to improve an answer.

Scoring Writing Tasks

The writing tasks in this workbook are scored based on rubrics that list the features expected of student writing. These features are based on the Common Core standards and are the same criteria used when scoring writing tasks on assessments. The rubrics used for scoring these questions are included in the back of this book. Use the rubric to score these questions, and as a guide for giving the student advice on how to improve an answer.

Practice Set 1

Task 1: Short Passage with Questions (Finland)

Core Writing Skills Practice

Core skill: Conduct short research projects that build knowledge about a topic.

Answer: The student should list the countries Russia, Ukraine, France, Spain, Sweden, Norway, Germany, Finland, Poland, and Italy.

Q1. Give a score of 0, 1, or 2 based on how many facts are correctly listed.
- The facts include that it is at the top of Europe, that the total area is over 130,000 square miles, that Finland is the eighth largest country in Europe, that its neighbors are Sweden, Norway, and Russia, that the capital is Helsinki, that the population is just over 5 million, and that people most commonly speak Finnish or Swedish.

Q2. Give a score of 0, 1, or 2 based on how well the answer meets the criteria listed.
- It may explain that the map shows that Finland's neighbors are Sweden, Russia, and Norway. It may also explain that Finland is in Europe or that Helsinki is the capital.

Task 2: Short Passage with Questions (Busy Bees)

Core Writing Skills Practice

Core skill: Recall information from experiences or gather information from print and digital sources; take brief notes on sources and sort evidence into provided categories.

Answer: The student should relate the information in the box to paragraph 3 and explain how the information tells how or why bees pollinate flowers.

Q1. Give a score of 0, 1, or 2 based on how many uses are correctly listed.
- The uses listed should be making honey and making beeswax.

Q2. Give a score of 0, 1, or 2 based on how well the answer meets the criteria listed.
- It should explain that the graph shows that only a small number of species of bees are honey bees.
- It may refer to the passage stating that only seven of the twenty thousand species of bees are honey bees.

Task 3: Long Passage with Essay Question

Use the Informative/Explanatory Writing Rubric to review the work and give a score out of 4.

Task 4: Personal Narrative Writing Task

Use the Narrative Writing Rubric to review the work and give a score out of 4.

Practice Set 2

Task 1: Short Passage with Questions (The Zoo)

Core Writing Skills Practice

Core skill: Recall information from experiences or gather information from print and digital sources; take brief notes on sources and sort evidence into provided categories.

Answer: The student may describe the dark scaly skin, the beady eyes, the long white teeth, or the jaws that can snap together.

Q1. Give a score of 0, 1, or 2 based on how well the answer meets the criteria listed.
- It should infer that it would not be safe for Fiona to have her hands near the fence as she may get bitten or hurt.
- It may refer to the details about the alligator having sharp teeth and snapping its jaws.

Q2. Give a score of 0, 1, or 2 based on how many correct details are given.
- The details given could be that it was big and fast, that it thrashed around when it was fed, that it had long sharp teeth, or that it snapped its jaws together wildly.

Task 2: Short Passage with Questions (Growing Pains)

Core Writing Skills Practice

Core skill: Write informative/explanatory texts to examine a topic and convey ideas and information clearly.

Answer: Use the Informative/Explanatory Writing Rubric to give a score out of 4.

Q1. Give a score of 0, 1, or 2 based on how well the answer meets the criteria listed.
- It should explain that a spider's exoskeleton is a hard skin on the outside of the body.

Q2. Give a score of 0, 1, or 2 based on how many boxes are correctly completed.
- The box for number of legs should be completed with eight legs.
- The box for body parts should be completed with two body parts.

Task 3: Short Story Writing Task

Use the Narrative Writing Rubric to review the work and give a score out of 4.

Task 4: Opinion Piece Writing Task

Use the Opinion Writing Rubric to review the work and give a score out of 4.

Practice Set 3

Task 1: Short Passage with Questions (Independence Day)

Core Writing Skills Practice

Core skill: Write informative/explanatory texts to examine a topic and convey ideas and information clearly.

Answer: Use the Informative/Explanatory Writing Rubric to give a score out of 4.

Q1. Give a score of 0, 1, or 2 based on how well the answer meets the criteria listed.
- It should describe one similarity between what the student does on Independence Day and what Tom does on Independence Day.
- It should use information from the passage and the student's personal experience.

Q2. Give a score of 0, 1, or 2 based on how many boxes are correctly completed.
- The box for Keith should be completed with "gives Tom an American flag."
- The box for Mr. Bennett should be completed with "plays the piano for everyone."

Task 2: Short Passage with Questions (Making Snowflakes)

Core Writing Skills Practice

Core skill: Write informative/explanatory texts to examine a topic and convey ideas and information clearly.

Answer: The student should describe a diagram that shows how to complete the project or how to complete a step in the project.

Q1. Give a score of 0, 1, or 2 based on how well the answer meets the criteria listed.
- The purpose of the passage should be to instruct or to teach how to do something.

Q2. Give a score of 0, 1, or 2 based on how well the answer meets the criteria listed.
- It should explain that the pencil is used to hold the snowflake up.
- It may describe how the string is tied to the pencil and the snowflake, and how the snowflake hangs down from the pencil.

Q3. Give a score of 0, 1, 2, 3, or 4 based on how well the answer meets the criteria listed.
- It should give an opinion on whether or not making a snowflake would be fun.
- It should use details from the passage to support the opinion.

Task 3: Long Passage with Essay Question

Use the Informative/Explanatory Writing Rubric to review the work and give a score out of 4.

Task 4: Personal Narrative Writing Task

Use the Narrative Writing Rubric to review the work and give a score out of 4.

Practice Set 4

Task 1: Short Passage with Questions (Neptune)

Core Writing Skills Practice

Core skill: Recall information from experiences or gather information from print and digital sources; take brief notes on sources and sort evidence into provided categories.

Answer: The student should explain that the numbers show The Great Dark Spot and the Small Dark Spot described in the passage.

Q1. Give a score of 0, 1, or 2 based on how many correct similarities are described.
- The similarities include that Neptune and Earth are both in the Solar System, both orbit the Sun, both have clouds, or both have storms.

Q2. Give a score of 0, 1, or 2 based on how well the answer meets the criteria listed.
- It should explain that Neptune is smaller than the other gas planets. It may also describe how Neptune is not as well-known or does not have rings like Saturn does.

Task 2: Short Passage with Questions (Fireworks)

Core Writing Skills Practice

Core skill: Write narratives to develop real or imagined experiences or events using effective technique, descriptive details, and clear event sequences.

Answer: The student should write a paragraph describing watching the fireworks from Julie's point of view. The paragraph should describe what she sees and how she feels scared.

Q1. Give a score of 0, 1, or 2 based on how well the answer meets the criteria listed.
- It should explain that the "million rainbows" describes the fireworks.
- It may explain that the author is trying to help readers imagine how bright, colorful, or amazing the fireworks were.

Q2. Give a score of 0, 1, or 2 based on how well the answer meets the criteria listed.
- It should explain that Julie feels scared and dislikes the loud noises.
- It may explain that Julie feels better when her mother squeezes her hand.

Task 3: Opinion Piece Writing Task

Use the Opinion Writing Rubric to review the work and give a score out of 4.

Task 4: Short Story Writing Task

Use the Narrative Writing Rubric to review the work and give a score out of 4.

Practice Set 5

Task 1: Short Passage with Questions (Plastics)

Core Writing Skills Practice

Core skill: Write opinion pieces on topics or texts, supporting a point of view with reasons.

Answer: Use the Opinion Writing Rubric to give a score out of 4.

Q1. Give a score of 0, 1, or 2 based on how well the answer meets the criteria listed.
- The boxes should have 80% for newspapers and 70% for fiberboard.
- The answer should explain how it shows that plastics are recycled much less.

Q2. Give a score of 0, 1, or 2 based on how many correct reasons are described.
- The reasons include that it has to be sorted into its different types and that many plastics have colors in them.

Task 2: Short Passage with Questions (Australia)

Core Writing Skills Practice

Core skill: Recall information from experiences or gather information from print and digital sources; take brief notes on sources and sort evidence into provided categories.

Answer: The answers are Western Australia (WA), Australian Capital Territory (ACT), Tasmania (TAS), and Queensland (QLD).

Q1. Give a score of 0, 1, or 2 based on how well the answer meets the criteria listed.
- It should infer that people moved to Australia after gold was discovered, and so Australia grew.

Q2. Give a score of 0, 1, or 2 based on how well the answer meets the criteria listed.
- It should describe two differences between New South Wales and the Australian Capital Territory.
- It may describe how New South Wales has a larger area based on the map, how New South Wales has more people based on the population numbers from the table, or how New South Wales is a state rather than a territory.
- It may also describe how New South Wales has the largest city, and how the Australian Capital Territory has the capital city.

Task 3: Long Passage with Essay Question

Use the Opinion Writing Rubric to review the work and give a score out of 4.

Task 4: Personal Narrative Writing Task

Use the Narrative Writing Rubric to review the work and give a score out of 4.

Practice Set 6

Task 1: Short Passage with Questions (A Tasty Trick)

Core Writing Skills Practice

Core skill: Recall information from experiences or gather information from print and digital sources; take brief notes on sources and sort evidence into provided categories.

Answer: The student may refer to how vegetables keep the body healthy, to the father worrying about the daughter getting sick, or to how the daughter now likes vegetables.

Q1. Give a score of 0, 1, or 2 based on how well the answer meets the criteria listed.
- It should relate the title of the passage to the events of the passage.
- It may refer to how the narrator's father tricked her or how the passage describes how the narrator began to find vegetables tasty.

Q2. Give a score of 0, 1, or 2 based on how well the answer meets the criteria listed.
- It should explain that the father started to sneak vegetables into different dishes.

Task 2: Short Passage with Questions (Recycle Today)

Core Writing Skills Practice

Core skill: Write opinion pieces on topics or texts, supporting a point of view with reasons.

Answer: The student should state an opinion and provide a reasonable explanation that tells why he or she feels that way.

Q1. Give a score of 0, 1, or 2 based on how many missing steps are correctly completed.
- The missing steps should be that the materials are sorted, and that the materials are cleaned.

Q2. Give a score of 0, 1, or 2 based on how well the answer meets the criteria listed.
- It should explain that the main purpose of the passage is to persuade readers.
- It may describe how the author wants people to recycle materials.

Task 3: Short Story Writing Task

Use the Narrative Writing Rubric to review the work and give a score out of 4.

Task 4: Opinion Piece Writing Task

Use the Opinion Writing Rubric to review the work and give a score out of 4.

Practice Set 7

Task 1: Short Passage with Questions (View from the Moon)

Core Writing Skills Practice

Core skill: Write opinion pieces on topics or texts, supporting a point of view with reasons.

Answer: The student should give plausible reasons that people want to visit the Great Wall of China. The reasons could be based on the information given in the passage, or on the student's own ideas.

Q1. Give a score of 0, 1, or 2 based on how well the answer meets the criteria listed.
- It should identify that the main idea is that the Great Wall of China cannot actually be seen from the Moon.

Q2. Give a score of 0, 1, or 2 based on how well the answer meets the criteria listed.
- It should identify that continents, oceans, and cloud cover can be seen from the Moon.
- It should identify that motorways, cities, landmarks, fields of crops, and the Great Wall of the China can be viewed from space.

Task 2: Short Passage with Questions (Comets)

Core Writing Skills Practice

Core skill: Write informative/explanatory texts to examine a topic and convey ideas and information clearly.

Answer: Use the Informative/Explanatory Writing Rubric to give a score out of 4.

Q1. Give a score of 0, 1, or 2 based on how well the answer meets the criteria listed.
- It should explain that comets appear to have a tail because the ice starts to melt, and this causes a trail to form behind them.

Q2. Give a score of 0, 1, or 2 based on how well the answer meets the criteria listed.
- It should identify that comets come from the Kuiper Belt, which is just past Neptune.
- It should identify that comets come from the Oort Cloud, which is out past Pluto.

Task 3: Long Passage with Essay Question

Use the Narrative Writing Rubric to review the work and give a score out of 4.

Task 4: Explanatory Writing Task

Use the Informative/Explanatory Writing Rubric to review the work and give a score out of 4.

Practice Set 8

Task 1: Short Passage with Questions (Better Than Expected)

Core Writing Skills Practice

Core skill: Recall information from experiences or gather information from print and digital sources; take brief notes on sources and sort evidence into provided categories.

Answer: The student should describe how Rat judges Cat when she expects that Cat wants to harm her, and relate this to the lesson of not judging others.

Q1. Give a score of 0, 1, or 2 based on how well the answer meets the criteria listed.
- It should explain that the end is a surprise because you do not expect the cat to be nice to the rat or want to help. It may describe how you would expect the cat to chase the rat.

Q2. Give a score of 0, 1, or 2 based on how well the answer meets the criteria listed.
- It should give details that show that the events could not really happen.
- The details given should be based on the way that the rat and the cat seem like human characters, including that they talk.

Task 2: Short Passage with Questions (Rookie)

Core Writing Skills Practice

Core skill: Write narratives to develop real or imagined experiences or events using effective technique, descriptive details, and clear event sequences.

Answer: The student should describe a time when he or she learned something new and tell whether it was a fun or difficult experience.

Q1. Give a score of 0, 1, or 2 based on how well the answer meets the criteria listed.
- It should explain that the narrator is told to take basketball more seriously because he keeps laughing about bouncing being called dribbling.

Q2. Give a score of 0, 1, or 2 based on how well the answer meets the criteria listed.
- It should tell how the narrator is describing how the basketballs were going everywhere.

Q3. Give a score of 0, 1, 2, 3, or 4 based on how well the answer meets the criteria listed.
- It should give an opinion on whether or not the narrator enjoyed basketball practice.
- It may describe how the narrator was laughing, seemed happy that he scored three baskets, or how he says that he is excited about being good enough to play his first game.

Task 3: Opinion Piece Writing Task

Use the Opinion Writing Rubric to review the work and give a score out of 4.

Task 4: Short Story Writing Task

Use the Narrative Writing Rubric to review the work and give a score out of 4.

Practice Set 9

Task 1: Short Passage with Questions (Take a Deep Breath)

Core Writing Skills Practice

Core skill: Conduct short research projects that build knowledge about a topic.

Answer: The student should research and describe how the heart and lungs work together. The answer should refer to how the lungs take in oxygen and how the heart pumps the blood to move the oxygen through the body.

Q1. Give a score of 0, 1, or 2 based on how well the answer meets the criteria listed.

- It should explain that the main purpose of the information in the box is to explain to readers how to take care of their lungs, or to persuade readers to exercise to keep their lungs healthy.

Q2. Give a score of 0, 1, or 2 based on how many purposes are correctly described.

- The purposes include taking in oxygen from the air, moving carbon dioxide out of the body, protecting the heart from shocks to the chest, and filtering blood clots.

Task 2: Short Passage with Questions (Making a Peg Doll)

Core Writing Skills Practice

Core skill: Recall information from experiences or gather information from print and digital sources; take brief notes on sources and sort evidence into provided categories.

Answer: The student should describe how the clothes pins have the basic shape of a person either by describing it in words or by labeling the diagram.

Q1. Give a score of 0, 1, or 2 based on how many items are correctly listed.

- The items that should be listed are a marker, a pipe cleaner, fabric, and wool.

Q2. Give a score of 0, 1, or 2 based on how well the answer meets the criteria listed.

- It should give an opinion on whether or not the student would like to make a peg doll.
- It should use information from the passage to support the opinion.

Task 3: Long Passage with Essay Question

Use the Informative/Explanatory Writing Rubric to review the work and give a score out of 4.

Task 4: Explanatory Writing Task

Use the Informative/Explanatory Writing Rubric to review the work and give a score out of 4.

Practice Set 10

Task 1: Short Passage with Questions (Pizza Night)

Core Writing Skills Practice

Core skill: Write informative/explanatory texts to examine a topic and convey ideas and information clearly.

Answer: The student should state a favorite food and explain why that food is liked.

Q1. Give a score of 0, 1, or 2 based on how many boxes are correctly completed.
- The box for Dad should be completed with pepperoni.
- The box for Mom should be completed with cheese.

Q2. Give a score of 0, 1, or 2 based on how well the answer meets the criteria listed.
- It should explain that Sandy likes the sweet pineapple.
- It should explain that Sandy likes that the pizza never has onion on it.

Task 2: Short Passage with Questions (Friends in Far Places)

Core Writing Skills Practice

Core skill: Write opinion pieces on topics or texts, supporting a point of view with reasons.

Answer: The student should argue that writing letters is important and tell what makes writing letters special.

Q1. Give a score of 0, 1, or 2 based on how many topics are correctly listed.
- The topics listed should be school, pets, families, and sport.

Q2. Give a score of 0, 1, or 2 based on how well the answer meets the criteria listed.
- It should give an opinion on whether or not the student would like to have a pen pal.
- It should give reasons to support the opinion.

Task 3: Short Story Writing Task

Use the Narrative Writing Rubric to review the work and give a score out of 4.

Task 4: Opinion Piece Writing Task

Use the Opinion Writing Rubric to review the work and give a score out of 4.

INFORMATIVE/EXPLANATORY WRITING RUBRIC

This writing rubric is based on the Common Core standards and describes the features that are expected in student writing. Give students a score out of 4 based on how well the answer meets the criteria. Then average the scores to give a total score out of 4. Students can also be given feedback and guidance based on the criteria below.

	Score	Notes
Organization and Purpose To receive a full score, the response will: • have an opening that introduces the topic • have a clear focus • be well-organized with related information grouped together • provide a concluding statement or section		
Evidence and Elaboration To receive a full score, the response will: • develop the topic with facts, details, or examples • include relevant text-based evidence when appropriate		
Written Expression To receive a full score, the response will: • be clear and easy to understand • have good transitions between ideas • use language to communicate ideas effectively		
Writing Conventions To receive a full score, the response will: • have few or no spelling errors • have few or no grammar errors • have few or no capitalization errors • have few or no punctuation errors		
Total Score		

OPINION WRITING RUBRIC

This writing rubric is based on the Common Core standards and describes the features that are expected in student writing. Give students a score out of 4 based on how well the answer meets the criteria. Then average the scores to give a total score out of 4. Students can also be given feedback and guidance based on the criteria below.

	Score	Notes
Organization and Purpose To receive a full score, the response will: • have an opening that introduces the topic and states an opinion • have a clear focus • be well-organized with related information grouped together • provide a concluding statement or section		
Evidence and Elaboration To receive a full score, the response will: • provide reasons to support the opinion • develop the topic with facts, details, or examples • include relevant text-based evidence when appropriate		
Written Expression To receive a full score, the response will: • be clear and easy to understand • have good transitions between ideas • use language to communicate ideas effectively		
Writing Conventions To receive a full score, the response will: • have few or no spelling errors • have few or no grammar errors • have few or no capitalization errors • have few or no punctuation errors		
Total Score		

NARRATIVE WRITING RUBRIC

This writing rubric is based on the Common Core standards and describes the features that are expected in student writing. Give students a score out of 4 based on how well the answer meets the criteria. Then average the scores to give a total score out of 4. Students can also be given feedback and guidance based on the criteria below.

	Score	Notes
Organization and Purpose To receive a full score, the response will: • have an effective opening that introduces the situation, characters, or event • have a logical and organized event sequence • have an effective ending		
Development and Elaboration To receive a full score, the response will: • have clearly developed characters, setting, and events • use dialogue and descriptions effectively • use narrative techniques effectively • have an appropriate style		
Written Expression To receive a full score, the response will: • be clear and easy to understand • have good transitions between ideas • use language to communicate ideas effectively		
Writing Conventions To receive a full score, the response will: • have few or no spelling errors • have few or no grammar errors • have few or no capitalization errors • have few or no punctuation errors		
Total Score		

Made in United States
Troutdale, OR
03/04/2025

29500876R00077